MARIE-PIERRE MOINE'S FRENCH KITCHEN

SALADS

LES SALADES

ILLUSTRATED BY NADINE WICKENDEN

SIMON & SCHUSTER
New York   London   Toronto   Sydney   Tokyo   Singapore

For my niece Clémence. Happy salad days.

SIMON & SCHUSTER
Rockefeller Center
1230 Avenue of the Americas
New York, New York 10020

SIMON & SCHUSTER and colophon are registered trademarks
of Simon & Schuster Inc.

Designed by Andrew Barron & Collis Clements Associates
Typesetting by Dorchester Typesetting in England
Printed and bound in Italy by New Interlitho

10 9 8 7 6 5 4 3 2 1

Library of Congress Cataloging in Publication Data
Available on Request
ISBN 0-671-89659-8

CONTENTS

Introduction *4*

INTRODUCTION

No French meal is complete without a salad. The healthiest way in the French canon to start a meal is to eat a small plate of lightly dressed vegetables: carrots, cabbage, celery root, and tomatoes are great favorites. Some vegetables require a little preparation or light cooking: mushrooms are blanched and marinated, cucumbers thinly sliced and sprinkled with salt, leeks steamed until just tender.

Whereas first course salads have featured on the French menu for a long time, *salades composeés*, complex salads substantial enough to serve as a main course, are relative newcomers. They first appeared on the tables of bistros and cafés. The recipe sections of women's magazines soon took them up: my mother's collection of cuttings and recipe cards from the early sixties features a large number of s*alades composées*. Invariably, the editorial message was that these were easy dishes to prepare, pretty and bright to look at, healthily nutritious – in fact just what appealed to the new modern woman with less time to spend in the kitchen. Needless to say, many of the sixties' salads *à la mode* now seem fussy, dull and dated – canned corn appeared in every second or third recipe, closely followed by canned beanshoots, mushrooms, crab and vast amounts of pineapple . . . Revised *salades composées*, simpler, inspired by the traditional cooking of provincial France with a few judiciously imported ingredients and techniques, are still rapidly gaining popularity, with the ever growing trend toward lighter one-course meals.

And should the meal be salad-free, the main course will be followed by a small green leaf salad, *salade verte*, to refresh the tastebuds and cleanse the palate before the cheese or dessert course.

What do you need to make a good salad? First and foremost, the right ingredients. The word fresh comes to mind: crisply fresh vegetables and herbs; dried herbs and spices that haven't sat on the shelf for a year; small bottles of speciality oils that are kept in a cool dark place. Equipment is simple: a salad spinner; plenty of paper towels; kitchen scissors to snip ingredients, a pair of sharp knives, a small whisk, servers, a range of wide shallow bowls and attractive plates to serve the salads on. Techniques aren't complicated: salad ingredients bruise easily and should be 'handled' as swiftly and gently as possible. Rinse in plenty of cold water until clean. Drain and dry thoroughly. Season and flavor with a light hand, tasting as you go along in order not to overwhelm delicate textures and flavors.

———

To prepare the recipes in this book, you will need the following ingredients : groundnut oil or sunflower oil; fruity olive oil and ordinary light olive oil; a small bottle of walnut oil; red or white wine vinegar, both if possible; cider vinegar; sherry vinegar; raspberry vinegar, Dijon mustard; coarse-grain mustard; sea salt; coarse sea salt; freshly ground black pepper.

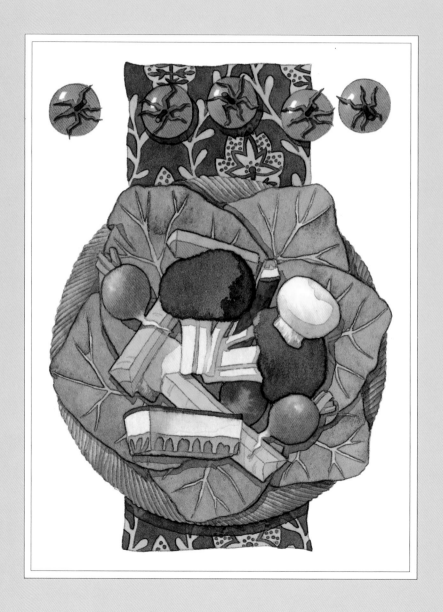

SAUCES ET CRUDITES

RAW VEGETABLES WITH SAUCES

As crunchy to eat as they sound, *crudités* are raw vegetables cut into small pieces – batons, florets, slices, trimmed leaves – and served as an *hors d'œuvre* with a bowl of dip. As an appetizer, they have to appeal to the eye and say "Eat Me" to the guests. I like to serve *crudités* in a pretty basket, perhaps on a bed of leaves, with an assortment of colorful dips. At the same time, have a bowl of olives flavored with olive oil and dried herbs, small croûtons and wedges of hard-cooked eggs or half-shelled quail's eggs on the table for a genuine feast.

Crudités are a cinch to prepare, as long as you have very fresh vegetables and a very sharp knife. Vegetable pieces should be bite-sized but substantial enough to pick up easily from the dish or basket. Leave cherry tomatoes, tiny button mushrooms, and fresh young radishes whole. Most sauces can be made and chilled well ahead. Cover *crudités* with a slightly damp dish towel or plastic wrap and leave them in the refrigerator or a genuinely cool place for an hour or two if it is convenient, but don't let them wilt and lose their crunch. Wait until the very last minute to display them: *crudités* age rather rapidly at room temperature.

MAYONNAISE

2 medium very fresh egg
yolks
1 tsp wine vinegar (red or
white)
1/2 tsp hot mustard
3/4 cup groundnut oil
1/2 cup light olive oil
sea salt and freshly ground
black pepper

To flavor:

1 tsp lemon juice
and, if you like, one of the
following:
finely snipped herbs –
chervil, chives, parsley,
tarragon
crushed garlic
finely chopped gherkins
anchovy paste
2 tbsp watercress, sorrel or
arugula, blanched for 30
seconds, then drained and
chopped
a touch of tomato purée for
color

What better way to start a selection of dip-in sauces for *crudités* than golden, wobbly, tempting, thick mayonnaise? The recipe below takes minutes to prepare and is guaranteed to work as long as your ingredients and equipment are at room temperature and the eggs you use are genuinely fresh. The flavorings are optional – green-flecked mayonnaise does look very appetizing in a plain china bowl.

★ Put the egg yolks, vinegar and mustard in a bowl. Cover and leave for at least 15 minutes. Have the other ingredients and equipment ready.

Put the bowl on a mat of a damp kitchen cloth, paper towel or dish towel – this will help hold it in place. Using an electric mixer, whisk the egg yolks, vinegar, and mustard until well mixed. Whisking constantly, trickle in the groundnut oil, one drop at a time to begin with, then a few drops at a time.

As soon as the mixture has really began to thicken, dribble in the oil a little faster, still whisking. Carry on whisking until you have worked in all the groundnut oil, then the olive oil.

Now taste your mayonnaise and season it with freshly ground black pepper, salt if needed, and a little lemon juice. Beat in 1 tablespoon of boiling water, this will help the mayonnaise keep stable. If you like, flavor the mayonnaise to taste with one or more of the suggested additions.

Cover with plastic wrap and chill until needed.

SAUCE AU ROQUEFORT

BLUE CHEESE DIP

Particularly good with cherry tomatoes, celery sticks, tiny florets of broccoli or cauliflower, and tiny button mushrooms. Incidentally, this dip doubles as a delicious sauce for pasta and steak, particularly hamburgers – prepare an extra amount and chill for 2 to 3 days until needed. I don't recommend freezing.

★   In a bowl, mash the blue cheese with a fork until soft. Work in the fromage blanc, yogurt, Tabasco, Worcestershire sauce, lemon juice, brandy (if using) and groundnut oil.

Taste and season with a little salt, if you like, and generously with pepper. If the mixture looks too solid, stir in a tablespoon or two more of yogurt or water.

Chill until needed. Season with a little extra pepper at the last minute.

2 oz roquefort, fourme d'Ambert, or other ripe blue cheese, crumbled
3 tbsp fromage blanc or light cream cheese
1 tbsp plain yogurt
a few drops of Tabasco sauce
a few drops of Worcestershire sauce
1 tsp lemon juice or white wine vinegar
2 tsp brandy (optional)
1 tbsp groundnut oil
sea salt and freshly ground black pepper

FROMAGE BLANC

SOFT CHEESE WITH HERBS

Worth trying with cucumber, crisp radishes and with thinly sliced rye bread (preferably buttered).

★   In a bowl, whisk the fromage blanc with a fork for a minute. Mix in the garlic, scallions and shallot.

Season to taste. Using a pair of scissors, snip in the chives and stir well. Chill for at least 1 hour or until needed. This dip is best eaten on the day it is prepared.

1 cup fromage blanc
1 clove garlic, crushed
white parts of 2 large scallions, finely chopped
1 shallot, finely chopped
a small bunch of chives
sea salt and freshly ground black pepper

ANCHOÏADE

ANCHOVY AND CAPER DIP

*12 anchovy fillets, drained
and chopped
4 tbsp fruity olive oil
2 or 3 tsp capers, drained
1 tsp Dijon mustard
½ cup fromage blanc, plain
yogurt or light mayonnaise
2 tsp lemon juice
freshly ground black pepper*

Makes a good spread for croûtons. Also try with broccoli florets and leaves of Belgian endive.

★   In a food processor, blend the anchovy with the olive oil for a few seconds. While still blending, add the capers.

Scrape the mixture off the sides of the bowl. Blend in the mustard, fromage blanc, and lemon juice. Season generously with pepper, taste and adjust the flavoring – add a little more fromage blanc if the mixture is too strong.

Spoon into a serving bowl and chill until needed.

CROUTONS

I frequently use croûtons in or with my salad recipes. They are easily made by cutting a slightly stale baguette into thin slices. Rub them lightly with the cut side of a garlic clove. If you like, sprinkle with a few drops of olive oil. Heat the broiler until hot, then reduce the heat and broil the croûtons until golden and crisp. Bite-sized croûtons are best if you first remove the crust. Croûtons will keep for a few days in an airtight container.

SAUCE AU POIVRON ROUGE

SWEET RED PEPPER SAUCE

Cut the peppers into strips. Coat them with the olive oil, then snip over a few basil leaves – the easiest way is to roll up the basil leaves into a tight little cigarette, then, using a pair of scissors, snip across into shreds. Sprinkle with the marjoram and garlic, season, stir, and set aside for a couple of hours. If it's convenient, chill overnight.

Blend the mixture in a food processor, then push through a sieve into a bowl – this is not absolutely necessary but it does refine the texture. Add the crème fraîche and mix in well. Adjust the seasoning. Snip over a little more basil and serve at room temperature.

3 large red bell peppers charred, skinned, and seeded
4 to 5 tbsp fruity virgin olive oil
a few leaves of fresh basil
½ tsp marjoram
½ clove garlic, crushed
sea salt and freshly ground black pepper
2 to 3 tbsp crème fraîche, cream cheese or fromage blanc

TAPENADE

OLIVE, TUNA AND ANCHOVY PUREE

*1 small can of tuna, well
drained and flaked
6 anchovy fillets, drained
and chopped
¾ cup black olives, pitted
2 tbsp capers, drained
3 cloves garlic, crushed
juice and 1 tbsp finely grated
zest of 1 unwaxed lemon
2 to 3 tbsp fromage blanc
2 to 3 tbsp extra virgin olive
oil
freshly ground black pepper*

This somewhat 'fishy' version of the traditional olive paste of Provence is less intense and very tasty. I serve it with cherry tomatoes, carrot, and cucumber sticks, croûtons or hard-boiled quails' eggs. Any leftover sauce will make an excellent salsa-style accompaniment to boiled or steamed new potatoes with grilled fish.

★ Put the tuna, anchovies, olives, capers, and garlic in the food processor. Mix until blended. Scrape the mixture off the sides of the bowl.

Add the lemon juice and zest with 2 tablespoons of the fromage blanc and olive oil. Blend together and season to taste, using plenty of pepper. If you like, blend in extra fromage blanc and olive oil.

ROUILLE

HOT CHILI PEPPER MAYONNAISE

This fiery dip from Provence makes a great all-purpose dressing. Try it with small batons of just ripe small raw zucchini. Use any leftovers to liven up soups, cold meats, and plain fish dishes.

★ In a bowl, mix the chili paste, moistened bread, crushed garlic, egg yolk and tomato purée. Season with a pinch of salt.

Put the bowl on a mat of a damp kitchen cloth, paper towels or dish towel to hold it in place. Using an electric hand mixer, whisk in a few drops of oil, as if you were making mayonnaise. Continue to dribble in the oil slowly, whisking steadily until the sauce thickens.

Adjust the seasoning. If you like a very hot sauce, add a little extra chili paste. Stir in a tablespoon of cold water. Cover and chill until ready to serve.

1 to 2 tsp chili paste
1 slice of soft bread, crust removed, broken into pieces and moistened with milk
2 to 3 cloves garlic, crushed
1 large very fresh egg yolk
1 tsp tomato purée
sea salt and freshly ground black pepper
¾ cup olive oil

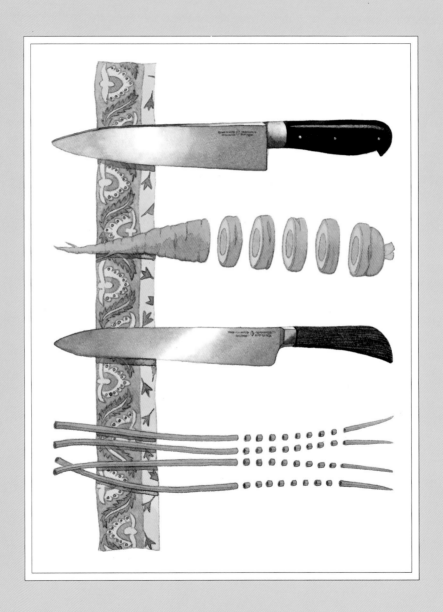

SALADES SIMPLES POUR COMMENCER

SIMPLE FIRST COURSE SALADS

French meals are less rigidly structured than they used to be, and much lighter, simpler affairs than the complex *repas* of yesteryear. Whereas *crudités* are really an *hors d'œuvre*, a little nibble to whet your appetite before the main meal, starter salads are the first 'proper' course of the lunch or dinner. In musical terms, if you think of the meal as a symphony, they would be the first movement – *crudités* and appetizers playing the part of the overture . . .

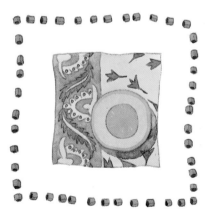

SALADE DE TOMATES A LA CIBOULETTE

TOMATO AND CHIVE SALAD

Serves 4

2 to 3 large or 4 to 5 medium ripe tomatoes, rinsed and patted dry
1 shallot, finely chopped
1 small bunch of chives
4 tbsp olive oil
2 tsp white wine vinegar or lemon juice
sea salt and freshly ground black pepper
fresh bread, to serve

This vibrant red salad is the freshest of summer starters. Use well ripened tomatoes. Chives and shallots are a pleasantly sharp combination which I sometimes replace with scallions, dried thyme and fresh basil.

★ With a sharp knife, cut the tomatoes into thin slices. Using a spoon, ease out the seeds and some of the white core with pale pulp. Discard.

Select an attractive round serving dish. Working from the center of the dish toward the outside, arrange the tomatoes in overlapping circles. Scatter the shallot over the tomatoes. Using scissors, snip half the chives over the lot. Season generously with salt and pepper.

In a cup mix the oil and vinegar. Season lightly. Sprinkle this dressing over the tomatoes. Snip over the rest of the chives. Leave at room temperature for a few minutes until ready to serve with plenty of good fresh bread to mop up the dressing and juices.

CAROTTES RAPEES

GRATED CARROT SALAD

This bright salad is my favorite way to eat vitamin-packed raw carrots and a perfect starter to a winter meal. For a more substantial salad, tuck in a few wedges of hard-boiled egg. A handful of raisins, hazelnuts or a few slivers of strong hard cheese are other nice optional extras.

★ Using the shredding disk of the food processor, grate the carrots. If you prefer to use a hand-grater, grate the carrots on the slant to get longer shreds.

In a cup combine the oil, orange juice, cilantro, lemon juice, and zest. Season to taste with salt and pepper.

Pour this dressing over the carrots and toss until the shreds are well coated. Leave to stand at room temperature for at least 20 minutes.

A moment before serving, toss in the parsley and olives. Adjust the seasoning. If you like, sprinkle in a few more drops of lemon juice and an extra trickle of oil to moisten the salad.

Serves 4

14 oz mature firm carrots, peeled
5 tbsp lightly flavored olive oil, or groundnut or sunflower oil, plus a little extra, if you like
1 tbsp fresh orange juice
½ tsp dried cilantro
1 tbsp juice and 1 tsp finely grated zest of an unwaxed lemon, plus 1 extra tsp lemon juice, if you like
1 generous tbsp finely snipped parsley
8 to 10 black olives, pitted and coarsely chopped
sea salt and freshly ground black pepper

CONCOMBRE A LA CREME ET AUX HERBES

CUCUMBER WITH CREAM AND HERB DRESSING

Serves 4

1 large firm cucumber, washed
1 heaped tbsp coarse sea salt
several sprigs of chives or fresh tarragon
1 tbsp lemon juice
1/3 cup crème fraîche or low fat crème fraîche
freshly ground black pepper

The technique of salting vegetables to get rid of excess bitter juices is known as *dégorger* and is very much part of French culinary grammar. The process takes a while – allow at least 40 minutes – but it works wonders for cucumber and produces a delicate dish with a subtle texture. Use the same method for large zucchini and eggplant.

★ Using a peeler or paring knife, peel off strips of cucumber skin at regular intervals all the way down the cucumber.

Now cut the cucumber into thin slices using a mandolin, your sharpest knife, or the food processor fitted with a thin slicing disk.

Place the sliced cucumber into a colander. Sprinkle with the coarse sea salt. Place a plate on top of the cucumber and put a weight on it. Leave to stand for about 1 hour.

Rinse thoroughly under cold water. Drain well, then press dry. Finish drying in a clean dish towel or with paper towels – the less moisture there is left in the cucumber, the finer the texture.

Put the cucumber in a serving dish. Using scissors, snip over the sprigs of chives or tarragon leaves, then sprinkle over the lemon juice. Mix well.

Spoon in the crème fraîche, tossing it well into the cucumber. Season with a little freshly ground black pepper, and chill for at least 30 minutes before serving.

SALADE DE CHOU

CABBAGE SALAD

Serves 4

*1 small head of white or red
cabbage, or a mixture,
quartered and cored
4 tbsp groundnut or
sunflower seed oil
2 tsp lemon juice
2 tsp orange juice
1 tsp mustard
1 tbsp mayonnaise
1/2 tsp dried thyme
sea salt and freshly ground
black pepper*

The crunch and flavor of raw cabbage never fails to take me right back to the lunches of my schooldays. The school I went to in Paris was literally around the corner from my parents' flat – I could see classrooms from our kitchen window and developed as a result a rather cavalier attitude to fine timing.

If you prefer, first blanch the cabbage in lightly salted boiling water. Drain well, then dry with a clean dish towel or paper towels. Peanuts or small cubes of broiled bacon (see page 32 *Salade verte aux petits lardons*) give extra bite to this salad.

★ Prepare the dressing. In a cup mix the oil, lemon and orange juice, mustard, mayonnaise, and thyme. Season generously with salt and pepper.

Using the shredding disc of the food processor, grate the cabbage. If you prefer, cut into long thin shreds with a sharp knife.

Put the cabbage in a bowl. Pour over the dressing. Toss the cabbage shreds until well coated. Leave to stand at room temperature for at least 20 minutes and adjust the seasoning before serving.

POIREAUX TIEDES A LA VINAIGRETTE

WARM LEEK SALAD WITH EGG AND SHALLOT DRESSING

Leeks are often referred to as *l'asperge du pauvre*, the poor man's asparagus. They are in fact a bit of a Cinderella : judiciously dressed and served warm, they taste like a million dollars but they will soon revert to a coarser flavor and texture if you leave them to get cold. This lovely warm salad is pretty enough to serve as a dinner party starter. I sometimes add a tablespoon of sautéed pine nuts to the vinaigrette dressing.

★ Steam the leeks over boiling water for 15 to 20 minutes until just tender.

Meanwhile make the dressing. Put the shallot in a bowl. Snip in a few sprigs of chives. Add a pinch of sea salt, the mustard, oil, and vinegar. Beat until the mixture emulsifies. Season to taste.

Finely chop the egg whites and push them through a small sieve. Mash the yolks and also push them through the sieve.

Leave the leeks until cool enough to handle, then lightly squeeze them to extract any excess moisture. Arrange 3 leeks on each of 4 plates.

Now dress the leeks. Spoon a little of the vinaigrette dressing over each serving. Sprinkle a band of egg yolk over the dressed leeks, then snip over a band of chives, then sprinkle over a band of egg white. Serve the dish while the leeks are still warm or at least tepid.

Serves 4

12 thin leeks, trimmed and washed

For the vinaigrette dressing:

1 shallot, very finely chopped
several sprigs of chives
sea salt and freshly ground black pepper
1 tsp Dijon or coarse-grain mustard
6 tbsp groundnut or sunflower oil
1 tbsp raspberry vinegar or 1½ tbsp white wine vinegar
2 hard-boiled eggs, shelled

SALADE DE POIVRONS

RED AND YELLOW BELL PEPPER SALAD

Serves 4

3 ripe unblemished red bell
peppers
1 ripe unblemished yellow
bell pepper
4 tbsp fruity olive oil
1 small clove garlic, crushed
½ tsp dried ground thyme or
ground coriander
1 tsp finely grated zest of
unwaxed lemon
1 tbsp white wine vinegar
sea salt and freshly ground
black pepper
a few leaves of fresh cilantro

From the Mediterranean, a colorful salad which will keep for 2 or 3 days in the refrigerator. I often add chopped avocado and a few black olives to the marinated peppers just before serving. This starter salad makes an excellent small side dish for roast or grilled chicken, especially after it has been left to marinate and mature for a couple of days.

★ Heat the broiler until hot. Broil the peppers until charred and blistering, turning them over to ensure even broiling. Leave until cool enough to handle, then peel off the skin. Pull out the core and cut open. Carefully remove all the seeds. Cut the peppers into long thin strips.

In a cup, mix the olive oil with the garlic, thyme or coriander, lemon zest, and 2 teaspoons of vinegar. Season with a little salt and pepper. Mix the strips of red and yellow pepper in a shallow dish. Trickle over the salad dressing, then stir well until the peppers are coated. Cover with plastic wrap and chill overnight or for several hours before serving.

Take out of the refrigerator at least 30 minutes before serving. Sprinkle with the rest of the vinegar and season to taste. Arrange the pepper strips attractively on a serving plate. Snip over a few cilantro leaves.

CELERI REMOULADE

CELERY ROOT SALAD

Serves 4

*about 1 lb celery root,
washed and grated or
shredded
1 tbsp lemon juice
fresh bread, to serve
sea salt and freshly ground
black pepper*

For the dressing:

*1 tbsp Dijon mustard
2 tsp white wine vinegar
1/2 cup mayonnaise (page 8)
a few sprigs each of fresh
parsley and chives or chervil*

T his velvety starter with a piquant edge is a great favorite with French gourmands. *Charcutiers* and *traiteurs* sell it by the tub at lunch time, doing a roaring trade, with very nice profit margins, thank you very much.

Blanching softens the texture but is by no means compulsory. If you are using bought mayonnaise, omit the vinegar.

★   If you prefer a softer texture, start by blanching the celery root. In a saucepan, bring lightly salted water to the boil. Sprinkle the celery root with the lemon juice and blanch for a few minutes. Drain well, refresh with cold water, drain again, and leave to cool.

While the celery root is cooling, prepare the sauce. Stir the mustard and vinegar into the mayonnaise. Snip in the fresh herbs and adjust the seasoning.

Squeeze the excess moisture out of the celery root with your hands. Dry with paper towels or a clean dish towel. If not blanching, sprinkle the celery root with the lemon juice before dressing.

Transfer to a serving dish. Spoon in a little of the dressing, stir well, then spoon in some more dressing – the celery root should be evenly coated with dressing.

Leave in a cool place for an hour, or longer in the refrigerator, stirring from time to time. At the last minute, adjust the seasoning. Snip over a few extra sprigs of herbs if you like. Serve with plenty of fresh bread.

SALADE DE HARICOTS VERTS AU FROMAGE

GREEN BEAN SALAD WITH A FRESH CHEESE DRESSING

E ven if they are going to be served cold, salads of cooked vegetables should be lightly coated with dressing while still warm. Whereas I am normally no great fan of trendy *Haricots verts croquants* – green beans, barely cooked and still on the hard side of *al dente* – I make a conscious effort to cook them that way when I prepare a salad. They will go on softening after they have left the pan and once they are dressed.

★ Bring at least 1 quart salted water to a boil in a large saucepan. Throw in the beans and cook at a rolling boil for 8 minutes or until just cooked but still crunchy. Drain, refresh with cold water, drain again and leave to cool a little.

After a few minutes, put the warm beans into a shallow serving dish. Sprinkle with about 1½ tablespoons of oil and ½ tablespoon of vinegar, toss and season lightly. Snip over a few sprigs of parsley and toss again. Set aside until ready to serve.

Meanwhile, prepare the dressing. In a bowl, mix together the scallion, garlic, and dried herbs. Season with pepper. Add the cheese, then the rest of the oil and vinegar. Mash well with a fork. Adjust the seasoning. Leave at room temperature until needed.

Spoon this cheesy dressing over the beans. If you like, snip over a little more parsley. Serve immediately, with garlic croûtons.

Serves 4

1 lb young green beans, topped and tailed
4 tbsp fruity olive oil
1½ tbsp white wine vinegar
a few sprigs of parsley
white parts of 2 large scallions, finely chopped
1 clove garlic, crushed
¼ tsp each ground dried thyme, sage and oregano
3 tbsp fresh ewe's milk or goat's cheese, crumbled
garlic croûtons, to serve (see page 10)
sea salt and freshly ground black pepper

CHAMPIGNONS A LA GRECQUE

MARINATED MUSHROOM SALAD

Serves 4

*1 lb button mushrooms,
wiped
1 tbsp groundnut oil
3 tbsp olive oil
white parts of 3 large
scallions, chopped
2 cloves garlic, crushed
12 coriander seeds
1 tsp ground cumin
1 tbsp juice and 1 tsp finely
grated zest of unwaxed
lemon, plus a few drops juice
to finish, if you like
2 tbsp dry white wine
a few leaves of fresh cilantro
or Italian parsley
sea salt and freshly ground
black pepper
warm bread, to serve
mixed salad leaves, to serve
(optional)*

Blanching the mushrooms lightens and refines their texture and produces a cleaner, lighter-tasting salad. Vegetables *à la grecque* – lightly cooked, then marinated with herbs, garlic and coriander – are a popular starter in France. Zucchini and onions can be prepared in the same way – allow an extra 2 minutes blanching time.

★ Bring some lightly salted water to the boil in a saucepan. Add the mushrooms and blanch for a minute, drain well and dry with paper towels. Cut the mushrooms into thin slices then transfer into a shallow bowl or dish.

Meanwhile, in a frying pan, heat the groundnut oil and half the olive oil over a moderate heat. Add the onion, garlic, coriander and cumin. Reduce the heat and sauté for 2 minutes, stirring well.

Now stir in the lemon juice and zest with the wine. Heat through. Season lightly. Pour the hot mixture over the mushrooms, stir in well, then sprinkle over the rest of the olive oil and stir again.

Cover, leave until cold then chill overnight. Take out of the refrigerator at least 30 minutes before serving. Stir and adjust the seasoning. If you like, sharpen the dressing with a few extra drops of lemon juice. Snip over a few fresh cilantro or parsley leaves. Serve with warm bread.

The marinated mushrooms look pretty and more substantial on a bed of mixed salad leaves.

SALADE DE FEUILLES DE CHENE AU BASILIC

OAK LEAF, TOMATO AND BASIL SALAD

Serves 4

1 large or 2 small ripe tomatoes, blanched, halved, seeded, skinned and diced
1 shallot, finely chopped
½ clove garlic, crushed
4 tbsp fruity olive oil
1 tbsp lemon juice
1 head of oak leaf lettuce, well trimmed, washed and drained
1 tbsp snipped fresh basil leaves
sea salt and freshly ground black pepper

For the goat's cheese toast (optional):

2 oz soft goat's cheese
1 tbsp olive oil
4 thin slices of baguette

Basil gives this fresh attractive salad a distinct aromatic edge. For maximum convenience, prepare the dressing and leaves ahead of time, leave in a cool place or chill until 20 minutes before serving. The goat's cheese toasts can be assembled early and broiled at the last minute. Save them for another occasion if the rest of the meal is very substantial and/or you are having a cheese course.

★ Prepare the dressing. In a wide, fairly shallow bowl, mix the diced tomatoes with the shallot and garlic. Season lightly. Pour in the olive oil and lemon juice. Toss, then season again.

Shred the larger of the lettuce leaves, cut off any tough ribbed central parts. Dress the salad.

If you are serving the salad with goat's cheese toasts, heat the broiler to high. In a cup, using a fork, mash the cheese with the olive oil until soft. Season with a little pepper. Spoon this mixture evenly over the baguette slices.

Reduce the heat and broil until golden and bubbly – this will take 3 to 5 minutes. Keep warm.

Just before serving, toss the salad. Scatter in the snipped basil leaves, reserving a few pieces. Divide the salad between four plates. Place one goat's cheese toast on each plate.

Season lightly and sprinkle over the rest of the basil. Eat as soon as possible.

SALADE DE CHAMPIGNONS ET DE CELERI-BRANCHE

MUSHROOM AND CELERY SALAD

A crunchy winter starter. Also try using the mustard and cream vinaigrette with Belgian endive and raisins.

★ In a shallow bowl, mix the mustard, vinegar, and shallot. Season generously, then whisk in the cream.

Cut the mushrooms into very thin slices. Sprinkle with lemon. Slice the celery very thinly.

Add the mushroom and celery to the dressing. Toss well to coat. Adjust the seasoning and sprinkle with chives. Toss lightly and serve as soon as possible.

Serves 4

1 lb white button mushrooms, trimmed, washed, and patted dry
1 tbsp lemon juice
1 head of celery, trimmed, washed, and drained
1½ tbsp finely snipped fresh chives

For the mustard and cream vinaigrette:

1 tbsp coarse-grain mustard
1½ tbsp wine vinegar
1 shallot, finely chopped
3½ tbsp light cream
sea salt and freshly ground black pepper

SALADES COMPOSEES

MAIN COURSE SALADS

With a few notable exceptions, such as *Frisée aux lardons, Salade niçoise,* and *Salade de foies de volaille, salades composées* were somewhat frowned on by purists until very recently. To this day one or two die-hards amongst the senior members of my own family never fail to remind me that *quelle salade!* means "what a mess" whenever I select an inspiring new concoction on a restaurant menu or – a greater crime still to put one on the table at home. My embattled relatives are struggling against the tide. A look at a few bistro menus soon shows that *salades composées* are an innovative and fast growing part of French gastronomy.

The following salads are substantial and balanced enough to be eaten as main courses. They also make satisfying snack meals and, in a number of cases using smaller helpings, appropriate dinner party starters.

SALADE VERTE AUX PETITS LARDONS

LEAF SALAD WITH BACON

Serves 2 to 3 as a main course, 4 as a starter

about 7oz salad leaves
3½ tbsp groundnut or
sunflower oil
7oz diced bacon, preferably
blanched (see below)
3 oz croûtons (page 10)
sea salt and freshly ground
black pepper
1½ tbsp red wine vinegar

Frisée aux lardons, curly endive with bacon pieces, is a universal French favorite and regularly features on the lunchtime menu of cafés and brasseries in towns all over the country. At its best, it is the most felicitous combination of fresh crunchy leaves and succulent hot bacon, but the average café's *Frisée aux lardons* is often a tough chew, with too many spiky curls, too much vinegar, and tiny mean bits of cold bacon. . .

Much better to have it at home. It only takes minutes to prepare and makes a splendid lunch. *A la maison*, I avoid curly endive and combine instead tender and sharp leaves: lettuce, oak leaf, a little baby spinach, arugula or sorrel, a few sprigs of flat-leaf parsley. If you prefer a single leaf, romaine, oak leaf, or batavia have the best texture for the job.

In France, to make succulent little lardons, I chop a thick slice of smoked pork belly: *poitrine fumée*. Elsewhere, my favorite alternative is to cut into small pieces thick slices of rindless smoky bacon. After years of snipping bacon straight into the pan, I have started to blanch it first. This may sound fastidious in the extreme, but I promise that it is a simple quick process and that you will notice the difference. Plunge your slices of bacon in a pan of simmering water, leave to bubble gently for 1 to 2 minutes, depending on thickness. Drain well and dry with a double layer of paper towels. Your bacon will be more tender, less salty and, best of all, will char and blacken less readily.

For this particular mixed salad, croûtons are a must (page 10), poached eggs and/or chopped avocado make optional extras if you are feeling very hungry. Eat this salad the moment you've finished cooking the bacon and you will not be disappointed. . .

★ Put the leaves in a shallow salad bowl. Sprinkle with 1½ tablespoons of oil and season lightly with salt and more generously with pepper.

Heat the rest of the oil in a small frying pan, reserving half a tablespoon. When the oil is hot, put in the bacon. Spread well and sauté over fairly high heat for 3 to 4 minutes, until the bacon is crisp and golden. Keep on stirring the bacon pieces during cooking to prevent them from burning. Reduce the heat a little after 2 minutes.

When the bacon is nicely browned, stir in the croûtons and the rest of the oil. Sauté for a minute, still stirring. Take the pan off the heat.

Pour the contents of the pan over the dressed leaves. Pour the vinegar into the pan, stir in well, then sprinkle the hot vinegar over the salad. Toss lightly, adjust the seasoning and eat immediately.

SALADE NIÇOISE

TUNA, EGG, AND TOMATO SALAD

Serves 2 to 3 as a main
course, 4 as a starter

2 large fresh eggs
3 ripe tomatoes, thinly
sliced, seeded and excess
pulp removed
½ cucumber, thinly sliced
7 oz baby lima beans, fresh
or frozen
7 oz small young green
beans, topped and tailed
white parts of 3 large
scallions, thinly sliced
½ small fennel bulb,
trimmed and chopped
(optional)
1 clove garlic, halved
1 head of lettuce, trimmed
and washed
1 medium can tuna, drained
and flaked
4 anchovy fillets, drained
and halved lengthways
about 12 black olives
sea salt and freshly ground
black pepper

For the dressing:

5 to 6 tbsp fruity olive oil
1½ tbsp white wine vinegar
sea salt and freshly ground
black pepper

The doyenne of French mixed salads, *Salade niçoise* should be made with very fresh ingredients and generously served in a shallow dish so that everybody can have a fair pick at all the nice bits and pieces.

★ Bring water to the boil in a saucepan and boil the eggs for at least 8 minutes. Sprinkle with salt and scatter over the sliced tomatoes and cucumber and set aside in a cool place.

Bring plenty of water to the boil in a separate pan, season with a little salt and add the lima beans, then the green beans. Boil over a fairly high heat for about 10 minutes, until done to your liking.

Make the dressing. In a cup beat together the oil and vinegar. Season lightly with salt and more generously with pepper.

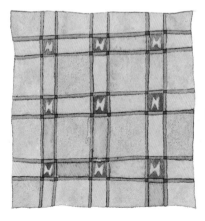

Once the eggs are cooked, drain them, refresh in cold water and crack the shells. Leave until cool enough to handle, then shell and quarter them lengthwise into wedges. Also drain and refresh the beans. Leave to cool for a few minutes. Put into a bowl (or return to the rinsed-out pan). Season lightly, then sprinkle over $1\frac{1}{2}$ tablespoons of dressing. Scatter over the onion, and the fennel, if using. Toss well to mix and set aside.

Now rub a serving dish with the cut sides of the garlic – choose one that is wide and fairly shallow. Put the lettuce leaves in the bowl, sprinkle with 1 tablespoon of dressing and toss lightly. Spoon over the beans.

Drain the cucumber and tomatoes, pat with paper towels to absorb salty juices and arrange on top of the salad. Scatter the tuna, anchovy, and olives over the salad. Season with a little pepper. Tuck in the wedges of egg around the dish and sprinkle with the rest of the dressing.

Adjust the seasoning and serve as soon as possible.

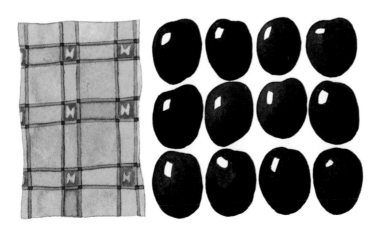

SALADE AUX FOIES DE VOLAILLE

CHICKEN LIVERS AND WALNUT SALAD

Serves 2 to 3 as a main
course, 4 to 5 as a starter

*1 head of lettuce, trimmed
and washed*
*3½ oz tender small spinach
leaves or arugula, ribbed and
washed*
*a handful of reddish or
brown salad leaves: red
batavia, oak leaf, shredded
trevisa, red Belgian endive,
trimmed and washed*
*1 small to medium red
onion, cut into very thin
rings*
*shelled kernels from 8 fresh
walnuts or pecans*
3½ oz fresh chicken livers
2 tsp groundnut oil
2 tbsp butter
*3½ oz diced bacon, blanched
and drained*
*sea salt and freshly ground
black pepper*

For the walnut vinaigrette:

2 tbsp walnut oil
1½ tbsp groundnut oil
*1½ tbsp raspberry or sherry
vinegar*

I first ate this salad (or a close relative of it) in south west France where poultry and walnuts are much-loved ingredients.
★ Arrange the lettuce and spinach leaves and onion rings on suitable individual plates. Scatter over the walnut kernels.

Make the dressing. In a cup, mix together the oils and vinegar until the mixture emulsifies. Season lightly.

Now prepare the chicken livers. Rinse them well, pat dry with a double layer of paper towels. At a slanting angle, cut into strips.

Heat the oil in a small frying pan over a moderate heat. Add the butter and swirl it around the pan until sizzling. Reduce the heat and lay the chicken livers in the pan, season lightly and cook for 1 minute, then turn over and cook for 1 minute longer.

Add in the diced bacon. Gently sauté for 2 minutes, then take the pan off the heat.

Divide the chicken liver and bacon between the plates, scattering the mixture attractively over the salad. Sprinkle with the dressing, adjust the seasoning and serve at once.

SALADE DU MARCHE

WINTER VEGETABLE SALAD WITH HAM AND CHEESE

Bring plenty of lightly salted water to the boil in a large saucepan. Add the potatoes, bring back to the boil and cook for 5 minutes. Add the mixed vegetables, return to the boil and cook for another 10 to 15 minutes until cooked through but still just a little firm.

Meanwhile, prepare the dressing: rub the egg through a sieve into a cup. Add the mayonnaise, crème fraîche, mustard, half the oil, and the vinegar. Beat until smooth and thick, then stir in the shallot and thyme. Season generously and set aside.

As soon as they are cooked to your liking, drain the vegetables in a colander, refresh them with cold water, and drain again. Leave for a few minutes, then return to the rinsed-out pan (or put into a bowl). Pour over the dressing, toss until well coated. Add the reserved oil to the now empty dressing cup. Season lightly.

Put the salad leaves in a shallow serving bowl. Sprinkle over the reserved oil and toss lightly. Using scissors, snip over the spring onions and half the chives.

Roll up each slice of ham into a cigarette shape. Snip this over the cooked vegetables. Now scatter the cheese over the lot and mix together gently. Heap the mixture in the center of the salad. Adjust the seasoning with a little extra pepper. Snip over the rest of the chives and serve as soon as possible.

Serves 4 as a main course

6 oz tiny new potatoes, well scrubbed
12 oz mixed vegetables: small cauliflower and broccoli florets, chopped celery, small carrots, baby turnips
3½ oz mixed salad leaves, prepared: lettuce, arugula, lamb's mache, red batavia
2 small scallions
a small bunch of chives
4 slices of good roast or boiled ham
⅓ cup gruyere or mature cheddar, cut into slivers

For the dressing:

1 hard-boiled egg, shelled
3 tbsp mayonnaise
1 tbsp crème fraîche
1 scant tbsp Dijon mustard
2½ tbsp groundnut oil
1½ tbsp red wine vinegar
1 shallot, very finely chopped
1 tsp dried thyme
sea salt and freshly ground black pepper

SALADE DE CHOU-FLEUR AUX PETITS LARDONS

CAULIFLOWER AND BACON SALAD

Serves 2 to 3 as a main course, 4 as a starter

1 head of cauliflower, washed, trimmed and cut into small florets
8 to 12 large lettuce leaves
a few sprigs of chives
a few leaves of chervil or flat leaf parsley
1 tbsp groundnut oil
³/₄ cup blanched and diced bacon
sea salt and freshly ground black pepper

For the dressing:

2 tsp coarse-grain mustard
1 clove garlic, crushed
1 tbsp cider or wine vinegar
2 tbsp walnut oil
2 tbsp groundnut oil

This unusual winter salad sits prettily on a lettuce *chiffonade*, a bed of loosely shredded leaves. It makes a nice main course after a filling starter – like fish stew or *Moules marinières*.

★ In a large saucepan, bring plenty of lightly salted water to a boil. Add the cauliflower and cook for 5 to 6 minutes – it should remain crunchy. Drain well in a colander. Set aside for a few minutes until the cauliflower stops steaming.

While the cauliflower is cooking, mix together the ingredients for the dressing in a large bowl and season generously. Tightly roll up the lettuce leaves and, using scissors, snip onto individual plates. Snip over a few sprigs of chives and scatter over a few chervil or parsley leaves.

Put the cauliflower in the bowl with the dressing and very gently toss until coated. Arrange on the lettuce *chiffonade*. Reserve.

Heat the oil in a small frying pan. Add the bacon and sauté over a moderate heat for 2 minutes, stirring frequently. Spoon over the cauliflower. Adjust the seasoning, snip over a few more chives and serve at once.

SALADE DE POMMES DE TERRE AUX MOULES

MUSSEL AND POTATO SALAD

Serves 4 as a main course

2 lb fresh mussels, well
scrubbed
2 shallots, finely chopped
1 cup dry white wine
1 tsp dried thyme
a few sprigs of parsley
6 black peppercorns
fresh bread and unsalted
butter, to serve
sea salt and freshly ground
black pepper

For the potato salad:

1 lb salad potatoes, well
scrubbed
1 shallot, finely chopped
4 tbsp groundnut or light
olive oil
several sprigs of parsley
1 tbsp wine vinegar, red or
white
1 generous tbsp crème fraîche,
or sour cream

Mussels and potatoes complement each other deliciously in this robust salad from northern France. If the recipe seems on the long side, it is simply because it combines two classic French *recettes de base*. Cook the mussels on their own, and, *voilà*, you have proper *Moules marinières*. The *Salade de pommes de terre* is also worth preparing in its own right – simply replace the mussel liquid with a tablepoon or two of cream or mayonnaise, and snip over a little extra parsley before serving.

★ Cook the potatoes for the salad. Bring plenty of lightly salted water to a boil in a big pan over a high heat. Add the potatoes and return to the boil. Reduce the heat a little. Cover and cook for about 20 minutes, or until the potatoes are done but still somewhat firm.

Meanwhile, prepare the mussels: pour the wine into a large heavy pan. Add the shallots, herbs, and peppercorns. Cover and bring to a boil over a high heat. As soon as the mixture bubbles, add in the mussels and cover again. Cook the mussels for 4 to 7 minutes, shaking the pan several times, until the shells open. Put the mussels into a colander and leave until cool enough to handle. Reserve the cooking liquid.

Discard any mussels that haven't opened. Shell the rest, adding any juices to the cooking liquid. Keep the mussels warm. Pour the cooking liquid through a small sieve into a jug or cup. Sprinkle some of this over the mussels, reserving at least 2 tablespoons for the dressing.

Place the cooked potatoes into a colander, refresh and leave to drain for a few minutes. As soon as they are cool enough to handle, peel the potatoes and cut into thick slices.

Prepare the dressing while the potatoes are cooling. In a cup mix the shallot and oil with 2 tablespoons of mussel liquid. Snip in plenty of parsley. Add the vinegar and crème fraîche, then whisk well and season generously.

Place the potatoes into a serving bowl. Spoon over $2/3$ of the dressing. Toss lightly until the potatoes are well coated. Heap the mussels in the middle of the potatoes and sprinkle with the rest of the dressing. Serve warm, with plenty of bread and butter.

SALADE TIEDE DE FRUITS DE MER

WARM SEAFOOD SALAD

Serves 4 as a starter

½ lb baby squid, cleaned and prepared for cooking
4 tbsp light olive oil
½ tsp harissa or hot chili paste
1 large clove garlic, crushed
1 scant tsp finely grated fresh ginger
1 tsp finely grated zest and the juice of 1 unwaxed lemon
½ tsp each ground cumin and coriander
a small bunch of chives or 2 small scallions
12 large cooked shrimp, heads and shells removed
1 lb freshly cooked, shelled mussels
½ lb button mushrooms, wiped
3½ oz mixed salad leaves
sea salt and freshly ground black pepper
bread and butter, to serve

For this salad based on traditional Provençal seafood, I have borrowed some spices from across the Mediterranean. Harissa is the spicy hot chili paste of Morocco. It is available in tubes or cans in a number of specialist or ethnic stores – a little goes a very long way and a tube will last indefinitely in the refrigerator. The contents of cans are better transferred to a small sterilized screwtop jar.

★ Several hours before you intend to serve the salad (or the night before), slice the squid into thin rings. Put in a bowl with 3 tablespoons of olive oil, the harissa, garlic, ginger, lemon zest, 1 tablespoon of the lemon juice, the cumin, and coriander. Stir well, then snip in a few sprigs of chives or a scallion. Add the shrimp and mussels and stir again. Cover and chill until about 30 minutes before the meal.

Bring plenty of lightly salted water to a boil with 1 tablespoon of lemon juice. Thinly slice the mushrooms and blanch for a minute in the lemon water. Drain well and dry carefully with a clean dish towel or paper towels.

In a bowl, mix the salad leaves and prepared mushrooms with the rest of the olive oil and a few drops of lemon juice. Season lightly. Divide between individual serving plates.

Heat a non-stick frying pan over a fairly high heat. Turn down the heat a little, and add the marinated seafood to the pan. Sauté for 2 to 3 minutes, stirring several times, until piping hot and tinged with gold.

Divide the seafood between the plates. Adjust the seasoning, snip over a few chives or the rest of the scallions. Serve as soon as possible, with bread and butter.

SALADE DE LENTILLES AU SAUCISSON

LENTIL AND SAUSAGE SALAD

Serves 4 as a main course

1 tbsp groundnut oil
1 Spanish onion, finely chopped
1 clove garlic, crushed
a few sprigs of parsley
1/2 tsp dried thyme
12 oz blue-green lentils from Le Puy, or other good small dark lentils, rinsed and drained
1/2 lb saucisson à l'ail or ready to eat smoked sausage, sliced
sea salt and freshly ground black pepper

For the dressing:

1 shallot, finely chopped
2 tbsp olive oil
2 tsp red or white wine vinegar

This simple supper dish is typical of the cooking of *la France profonde*, the heart of the French countryside. The lentils of Le Puy in the Auvergne have an excellent texture and a fine flavor. Another way to enjoy this warm salad is to leave out the *saucisson à l'ail* and to serve it with top quality broiled country sausages.

★ In a heavy saucepan heat the groundnut oil. Add the onion and sauté for a few minutes over a low heat, stirring occasionally.

Stir in the garlic, a few sprigs of parsley and the thyme. Now add the lentils. Generously cover with water – there should be one inch of liquid above the lentils. Season lightly. Cover and simmer over a fairly low heat for 30 to 40 minutes, until the lentils are just tender but not soft.

Check and stir the lentils from time to time – you may want

to add a tablespoon or two of water if they look dry. Adjust the seasoning. Remove the sprigs of parsley and add the sliced sausage towards the end of cooking – it only needs time to heat through.

Prepare the dressing while the lentils are simmering. In a cup, combine the shallot with the oil and season with salt and pepper. Snip in plenty of parsley. Stir, add the vinegar and stir again.

Drain the lentils in a colander placed over a bowl to catch the cooking liquid – use for sauces or soups. Put the drained lentils into a serving dish. Drizzle over the dressing, toss lightly until coated. Serve warm.

This preparation will keep or a day or two in the refrigerator. Return to room temperature well before serving.

SALADES VERTES ET PETITES SALADES

GREEN SALADS AND SIDE SALADS

For the French, lettuce dressed with oil and wine vinegar is *la salade verte par excellence*, the little salad you eat after the *plat de résistance* to refresh your palate. The usual way to have it is on the main plate, but small side plates are produced for formal occasions.

Rule number one of a good green salad is that the leaves should be entirely free of moisture before dressing. My earliest memories of helping in the kitchen focus on vigorously shaking a wire basket full of freshly washed garden lettuce. When nobody was watching, I used to practice swinging the said basket at arm's length and making it do a complete turn – a modest kitchen equivalent of looping the loop. Needless to say, the pristine lettuce often ended on the floor. I now use a salad spinner, or rather two salad spinners, one large and one small, to extract every drop of water from the leaves. If I feel fastidious, I gently press the leaves in a clean dish towel or yet more lengths of my indispensable paper towels.

Another trick I learnt at an impressionable age was to use my hands (after quasi-surgical scrubbing, and only when entirely free of minor cuts and the like) to toss and coat a salad. I still find it the best method for large quantities. When dressing a green leaf salad for four or so people I use servers. The salad dishes of my youth were very deep, round earthenware bowls. I now prefer dishes that are shallower and help distribute the dressing lightly and evenly over the whole of the leaves.

TROIS PETITES LAITUES

Serves 4
*1 head of fresh lettuce,
rinsed and dried (see p 47)*

Three ways to dress a head of lettuce.

VINAIGRETTE CLASSIQUE

Standard Oil and Vinegar Dressing

*3 tbsp groundnut or
sunflower oil
a scant ¼ tsp mustard
1½ tsp red wine vinegar
sea salt and freshly ground
black pepper*

The amount below will dress a standard-sized head of lettuce. Vinaigrette can be made in bulk and chilled for up to two weeks.

★ Follow the same ratio of oil to mustard and vinegar and the same basic method. Chill the dressing in a clean screwtop jar for 30 minutes. Take out of the refrigerator. Whisk the dressing again vigorously until the mixture is well emulsified, then return the jar to the fridge.

Put the oil in a small cup. Season generously with salt. Beat with a fork, small whisk or teaspoon. Stir in the mustard, beat again, then add the vinegar, and beat again until emulsified.

Put the salad in a shallow bowl. Spoon the dressing over the salad, toss in lightly but thoroughly. Serve within minutes.

VINAIGRETTE A LA CREME

Creamy Dressing

This aromatic cream vinaigrette is particularly suitable for fine flavored or soft salad leaves.

★   In a shallow salad bowl, mix together the mustard, crème fraîche, lemon juice, and shallot. Season liberally. Snip in a half the chives and tarragon. Beat well.

Add the prepared lettuce to the bowl. Toss lightly, sprinkle in the rest of the herbs. Toss again. Adjust the seasoning and serve within minutes.

1 tsp coarse-grain mustard
2 scant tbsp crème fraîche
1 tbsp sunflower oil
2 tsp lemon juice
½ small shallot, finely chopped
1 tbsp snipped chives
2 tsp snipped tarragon
sea salt and freshly ground black pepper

ASSAISONNEMENT MIMOSA

Egg Dressing

This is a great all-purpose dressing, equally at home on soft lettuce and coarser, bitter leaves. A small handful of croûtons and a few thin little strips of drained anchovy are appropriate extra options.

★   Prepare the dressing: put the mustard and vinegar in a suitable salad bowl. Season and mix well. Beat in the oil until the mixture emulsifies. Set aside. Rub the egg whites through a sieve and reserve. Do likewise with the yolks.

Put the salad in the bowl. Toss lightly until coated. Sprinkle the salad with the rubbed egg whites and yolks. Scatter over the parsley and chives. Toss again delicately. Adjust the seasoning and serve within minutes.

1 tsp Dijon mustard
1¼ tbsp wine or cider vinegar
3 to 4 tbsp groundnut oil
2 fresh eggs, hard-boiled and shelled
1 tbsp finely snipped parsley
1 tbsp finely snipped chives
sea salt and freshly ground black pepper

POIS GOURMANDS EN SALADE

SNOW PEA SALAD

Thisdelicate spring salad is a good follow-up to a fish course. ★ Remove the strings from the snow peas. Bring plenty of lightly salted water to a boil in a large pan. Add the snow peas and boil for 5 minutes.

Serves 4

1 lb snow peas, tailed
several sprigs of chervil or
tarragon
sea salt and freshly ground
black pepper

For the dressing:

2 tbsp light cream
2 tbsp sunflower or
groundnut oil
1 tsp finely grated zest and
1 tbsp juice of an unwaxed
lemon

Drain. Refresh with cold water and drain again. Pat dry with paper towels or a clean dish towel. Put in a shallow salad bowl. Snip over the fresh herbs and season with a little pepper.

Make the dressing. In a cup mix together the cream, oil, lemon zest, and juice. Season lightly.

Sprinkle the dressing over the snow peas. Toss lightly until coated. Serve as soon as possible.

MACHE RAFRAICHIE

CHILLED MACHE

Serves 4

*7 oz trimmed and washed
mache salad
2½ tbsp fruity olive oil (or
1½ tbsp groundnut oil mixed
with 1 tbsp walnut oil)
sea salt and freshly ground
black pepper*

Rules are made to be broken. The French tend to dress their leaf salads at the last minute, so that the leaves stay crisp and firm. Not so mache, which tastes infinitely superior if you dress it, then leave it to chill, and marinate for a good 15 minutes. . . I am indebted to my father's brother for this recipe. He was in charge of lunch and produced a no-nonsense *déjeuner champêtre* for us all, happily sitting in his garden under the apple trees: chilled Charentais melon with a touch of sweet Vouvray wine, lamb brochettes (*mais oui*, the French have barbecues), yellow rice with saffron and onions, tomatoes stuffed with herbs. Then came the best mache salad I had ever eaten. What was the secret? "It is the easiest thing in the world," Oncle Jean said. "Don't use vinegar and leave the salad to rest in the refrigerator before serving."

A small handful of very fresh walnut or pecan kernels is an optional extra, but I find this palate-cleansing salad even more refreshing *au naturel.*

★   Pat the mache dry with paper towels or in a clean dish towel. If it is bunched up too tightly in big clusters, separate the mache into small manageable floret-sized bouquets.

Put the salad in a serving bowl. Sprinkle with one-third of the oil and season lightly. Toss together, then sprinkle with more oil and season again – very sparingly.

Toss and sprinkle with the rest of the oil – this way the salad will be evenly coated. Season again and chill for 15 to 20 minutes while you are eating the main course. Taste and adjust the seasoning just before serving.

SALADE PANACHEE DE PRINTEMPS

MIXED SALAD FOR THE SPRING

Serves 4

*hearts of 2 small lettuces,
rinsed, drained, and
separated into leaves
about 12 small leaves each of
young spinach and sorrel
6 small bunches of mache,
separated into tiny bouquets
1 tbsp snipped mint leaves
2 tbsp small ripe
strawberries
sea salt and freshly ground
black pepper*

Serves 4

*hearts of 2 small lettuces, 2½
tbsp sunflower or hazelnut
oil
2½ tsp sherry or raspberry
vinegar*

Panacher means to mix – poetically harping back to the multi-colored plumes of the knights of old. This deliciously sharp little spring salad is certainly packed with subtle flavors and textures.

★ Mix the leaves in a shallow serving bowl, reserving the strawberries. Season lightly, sprinkle over half the oil and half the vinegar. Toss to coat and season again lightly.

Season the strawberries with a little pepper. Scatter over the salad, sprinkle with the rest of the oil and vinegar. Toss delicately. Adjust the seasoning and serve as soon as possible.

SCAROLE AU GRUYERE

RED ESCAROLE WITH CHEESE

Serves 4

head of red or green escarole, trimmed and washed
2 oz gruyère cheese, cut into small slivers or diced

For the vinaigrette:

1 tbsp lemon juice
2 tbsp finely snipped chives
½ clove garlic, crushed (optional)
3½ tbsp fruity olive oil
sea salt and freshly ground black pepper

This is a good salad to serve if you want to skip the cheese course.

★ Prepare the salad leaves. Roll some of the larger leaves and snip them into strips. Loosely tear up the other leaves.

Mix the dressing ingredients in a shallow bowl. Combine the lemon juice with half the chives and the garlic, if using. Season generously and beat in the oil.

Put the salad leaves on top and scatter over the cheese. Toss lightly but thoroughly, then sprinkle the rest of the chives over the dressed salad. Serve as soon as possible.

SALADE D'ENDIVES A LA POIRE

BELGIAN ENDIVE AND PEAR SALAD

Serves 4

4 heads of white or red Belgian endive, washed and trimmed
1 large ripe pear, peeled, quartered, and cored
1 tsp lemon juice
½ tsp Dijon-style mustard
2 tsp cider vinegar, or a little more, if required
½ tsp honey
3 tbsp crème fraîche
sea salt and freshly ground black pepper

Unusual, and often my choice to follow a rich winter casserole.

★ Cut the bigger leaves of Belgian endive into ⅔ in segments. Leave the small leaves whole. Cut the pear into thin slices. Sprinkle the pear slices with the lemon juice.

In a shallow bowl, mix the mustard, cider vinegar, and honey. Season lightly, then beat in the crème fraîche. Adjust the seasoning – if you like, sharpen with a little extra cider vinegar.

Toss in the Belgian endive and pear. Arrange on 4 individual small plates. Sprinkle over a little extra pepper and serve as soon as possible.

LIST OF RECIPES